WORKING WITH FACTS & DETAILS

ALVIN KRAVITZ, Ed.D.
C. W. Post College

DAN DRAMER

THE MCP SKILL-BY-SKILL PROGRAM CONTAINS WORKBOOKS
IN THE FOLLOWING READING-SKILL AREAS:

Building Word Power, B-F
Working With Facts and Details, C-F
Getting the Main Idea, B-F
Increasing Comprehension, B-F
Organizing Information, B-F
Using References, C-F
Following Directions, B-D

Copyright © 1983, 1978 by MODERN CURRICULUM PRESS, INC.
13900 Prospect Road, Cleveland, Ohio 44136

All rights reserved. Printed in the United States of America.
This book or parts thereof may not be reproduced in any form or mechanically stored in any retrieval system without written permission from the publisher.
Published simultaneously in Canada by Globe/Modern Curriculum Press, Toronto.

ISBN 0-87895-343-4   1 2 3 4 5 6 7 8   85 84 83

TABLE OF CONTENTS

GETTING THE MOST FROM YOUR SKILLBOOSTER	3
FACT OR MAKE-BELIEVE?	5
KING ARTHUR	6
TWO STORIES	8
A REAL MYSTERY	10
POSTER FUN	12
FIND THE FACTS	14
THE GRAND CANYON	16
A BRIDGE OF FRIENDSHIP	18
GET THE PICTURE	20
A BRAVE PRINCESS	22
THE LONGEST DITCH IN THE WORLD	24
THE GREAT WALL OF CHINA	26
BUILDING A TREE HOUSE	28
ASKING IMPORTANT QUESTIONS	29
BIRD MAN	30
HARRIET TUBMAN	32
THE GREAT PYRAMID	34
THE LEANING TOWER OF PISA	36
INVISIBLE WRITING	38
FIND THE DIFFERENCE	40
TWO QUEENS	42
UNCOVERING HIDDEN FACTS	44
PUZZLING QUESTIONS	46
ANSWER KEY	47
SKILLS INDEX	Inside Back Cover

GETTING THE MOST FROM YOUR SKILLBOOSTER

WORKING WITH FACTS AND DETAILS IS IMPORTANT

Facts and details are all around you. You find them when you watch TV, listen to the radio, or talk with friends. You also find facts and details when you read a road sign, a menu, or a book.

Knowing how to recognize and use these small pieces of information can be fun and interesting. For example, in this book you will find facts about writing with invisible ink and taking a snapshot with a camera. As you do these pages, you will also find out about interesting people who really lived and about some of the world's most interesting places to visit.

FOLLOW DIRECTIONS CAREFULLY

Notice the details in the directions. You should make sure you understand them before you start to work. If they don't make sense, read them over again. If the directions don't make sense after reading them the second time, ask your teacher for help.

THINK AND WRITE

Take your time as you write the answers on the page. You will do a much better job if you work carefully and really *think* about your work.

CHECK YOUR WORK

When you have finished a page, you will want to know how many of your answers are correct. The answers for the exercises in this book are on pages 47 and 48. If it is all right with your teacher, you can use these answers to check your work.

LEARN FROM A WRONG ANSWER

If all your answers for an exercise are correct, you are doing a great job! But nobody gets all the answers right all the time. So, sometimes your answer will be wrong. When that happens, it is a good chance for you to learn something new. Here is a smart thing for you to do when you check your work. First check your answer with the answers at the back of the book. If you got an answer wrong, write a mark beside it. Here is the important part. After you have marked your wrong answer, check the back of the book again. Check to *find out what the correct answer is.* That way, the next time you are asked a question like the one that you missed, you will have a better chance to get the answer correct.

RELAX AND HAVE FUN

Doing the pages in this book will be fun. So relax, do your best and have fun working with facts and details.

Project Supervision: Dimensions & Directions, Ltd.
Illustration: Olivia Cole Hauptfleisch; Jack Clellan

Photos: EPA-Documerica;
11 British Airways; 17 Arizona Office of Tourism; 22 Culver Pictures, Inc.;
30 The New York Historical Society; 34 U.P.I.; 36 Venton Beals

FACT OR MAKE-BELIEVE?

Some of the word groups below tell about facts. A fact is something that is real. Other word groups tell about something that can only happen in a make-believe story.

DIRECTIONS: Write *F* in front of each group of words that give a fact. Write *MB* in front of each idea that could only happen in a make-believe story. The first one is done for you.

MB 1. a princess who slept for one hundred years

_____ 2. a girl who can make the sky turn green.

_____ 3. rain coming from the clouds

_____ 4. a wool shirt

_____ 5. a kite in the sky

_____ 6. a bear talking to the sky

_____ 7. a glass of milk

_____ 8. a duck with horns

_____ 9. a talking grasshopper

DISTINGUISHING FACT FROM FANTASY — 5

KING ARTHUR

Many people who study history are interested in reading about a king who lived long ago in the country of Britain. His name was King Arthur. King Arthur was a great hero. He was a good ruler of his country. He won some battles.

After Arthur died, many make-believe stories were told about his exciting adventures. Each new story made him a greater hero. Some stories tell that Arthur fought dragons and giants. The stories say that Arthur learned magic from a teacher named Merlin. Merlin also used his magic to help King Arthur to win battles. According to the stories, King Arthur married a beautiful princess named Guenevere. They lived in a castle called Camelot. Some tales say that Camelot was in Wales, on Britain's west coast. In other stories, the castle floated in the clouds.

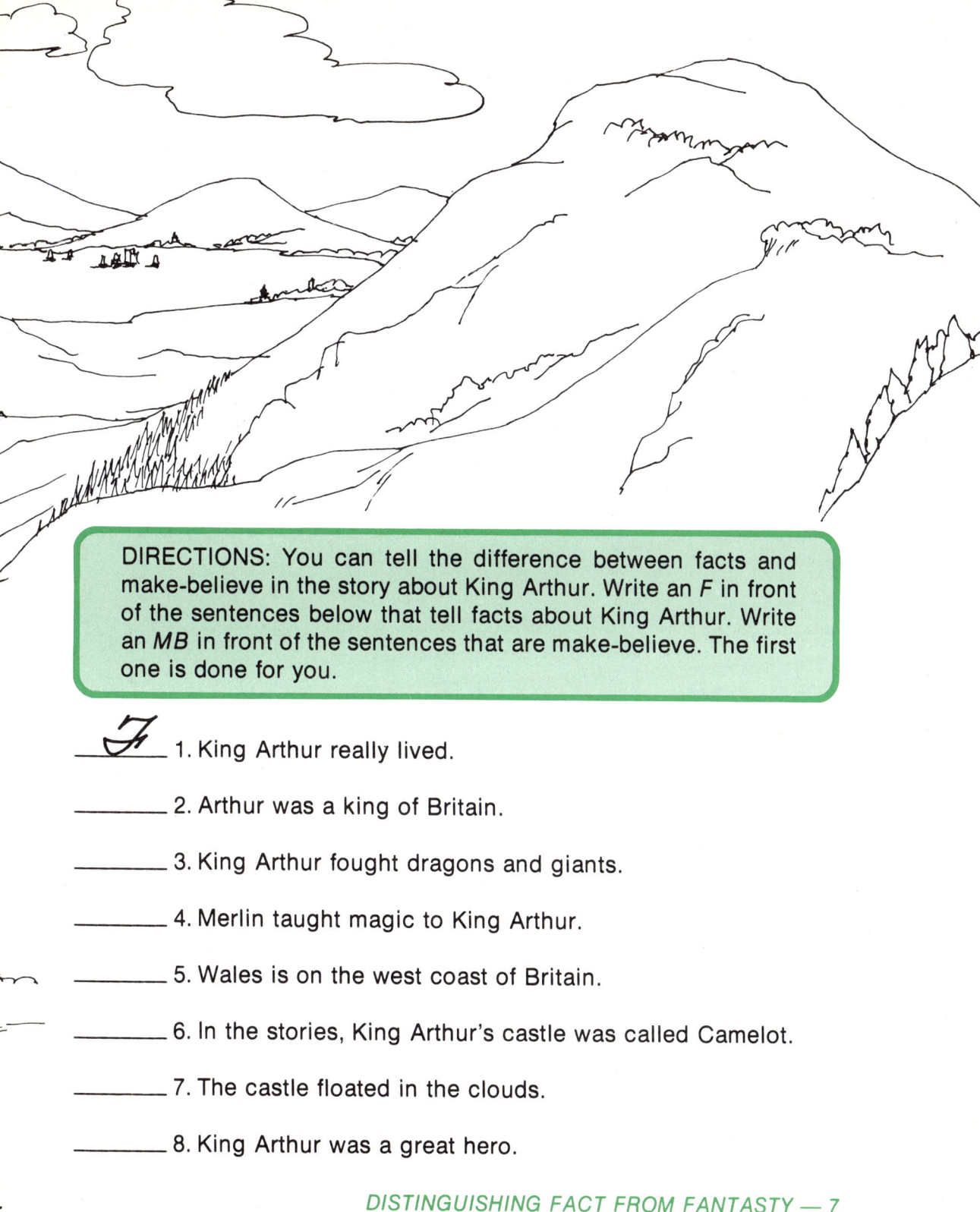

DIRECTIONS: You can tell the difference between facts and make-believe in the story about King Arthur. Write an *F* in front of the sentences below that tell facts about King Arthur. Write an *MB* in front of the sentences that are make-believe. The first one is done for you.

__*F*__ 1. King Arthur really lived.

_____ 2. Arthur was a king of Britain.

_____ 3. King Arthur fought dragons and giants.

_____ 4. Merlin taught magic to King Arthur.

_____ 5. Wales is on the west coast of Britain.

_____ 6. In the stories, King Arthur's castle was called Camelot.

_____ 7. The castle floated in the clouds.

_____ 8. King Arthur was a great hero.

DISTINGUISHING FACT FROM FANTASTY — 7

TWO STORIES

There are two stories on this page. One story tells facts about how chewing gum is made. The other story is make-believe. It tells about a piece of magic chewing gum.

> DIRECTIONS: Write *F* in the blank next to each sentence that tells facts about how gum is made. Write *MB* next to each sentence that comes from the make-believe story.

MB 1. Terry once got a piece of magic chewing gum.

F 2. Chewing gum is made from the sap of some trees that grow in South America.

_____ 3. After the workers get the sap, they boil it.

_____ 4. When Terry chewed the gum, everything he said sounded smart.

_____ 5. Terry told his parents how to fix their broken TV set.

_____ 6. Then the sap is mixed with flavoring and sugar.

_____ 7. He showed his teacher how to do some problems from her college arithmetic book.

_____ 8. The gum is then cut into small pieces.

_____ 9. After it is cut, the gum is ready to be chewed.

_____ 10. The magic only stayed in the gum for three hours.

_____ 11. When the three hours were up, Terry changed back into being a regular third-grade boy again.

You can write two stories by using the sentences from page 8. Write one story about how chewing gum is made. Write another story about Terry's magic chewing gum.

How Chewing Gum Is Made

___

___

___

___

___

___

Terry and the Magic Chewing Gum

___

___

___

___

___

___

DISTINGUISHING FACT FROM FANTASY — 9

A REAL MYSTERY

You know that a fact is something that is real. Facts can be checked and proven. Here is a fact: *It gets dark at night*.

Opinions are different from facts. An opinion is a belief or something a person thinks is true. An opinion can't be proven. Here is an opinion: *Someday people will live on Mars*.

> DIRECTIONS: As you read the report below, think about which ideas are facts, and which are people's opinions.

Stonehenge is in England. If you went there, you would see huge rocks standing silent and tall against the sky. The rocks are put in a circle. They have been standing that way for at least three thousand years.

People have different opinions about who built Stonehenge. Some stories say that it was built long ago by people called *Druids*. The stories say that the Druids worked magic. Another opinion is that Stonehenge was built by a tribe of men who lived long ago. These men were just learning how to use metal tools.

Another fact that no one knows is how Stonehenge was built. Each of the large stones in the circle weighs as much as three elephants. The builders of Stonehenge had to move these stones twenty miles to bring them to Stonehenge. No one knows exactly how the Stonehenge builders moved the stones. Some experts have an opinion that Stonehenge builders rolled the heavy stone slabs on logs like this:

The biggest mystery about Stonehenge is why it was built. We know that some early people of England prayed to the sun. So some people have the opinion that Stonehenge was built so that people could worship the sun.

A scientist once studied Stonehenge. He saw something surprising. He saw that the sun made some stones put shadows on other stones. He saw that the sunlight and shadows on the strange stones in Stonehenge could be used to tell the days of the year. They could also be used to tell when the seasons would change. This scientist's opinion is that Stonehenge is a big calendar.

> DIRECTIONS: Write an *F* on the line in front of each sentence that is a fact. Write an *O* on the line in front of each sentence that is an opinion.

_____ 1. Stonehenge is made of huge rocks that stand in a circle.

_____ 2. Stonehenge was built by the Druids.

_____ 3. The stone slabs were brought to Stonehenge by rolling them on logs.

_____ 4. Some people that lived in England many years ago prayed to the sun.

_____ 5. Stonehenge is really a big calendar.

DISTINGUISHING FACT FROM OPINION — 11

POSTER FUN

A — This is a dumb bunny.

B — You can't get very far unless you're willing to stick your neck out.

C — SWEETS + ◯ = DECAY

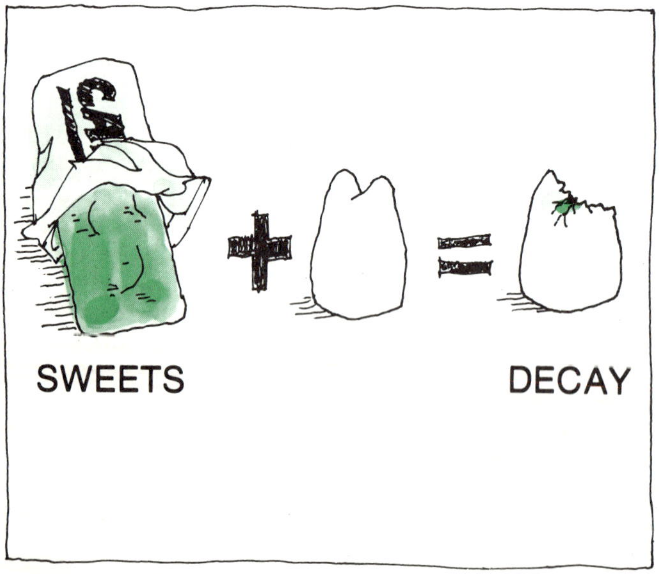

D — EAT OKAY SNACKS

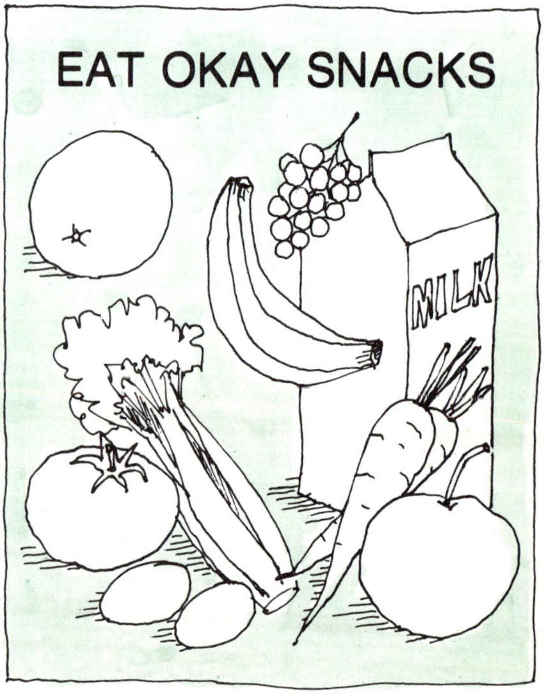

DIRECTIONS: Each poster on page 12 has a letter in the corner. Write the letter of the poster in the blank to answer each question below. The first one is done for you.

_B_ 1. Which poster has a turtle on it?

____ 2. Which poster tells you to cross on the green light?

____ 3. Which poster says that candy can hurt your teeth?

____ 4. Which poster says to eat healthful food?

____ 5. Which poster says it may sometimes be all right to take a chance?

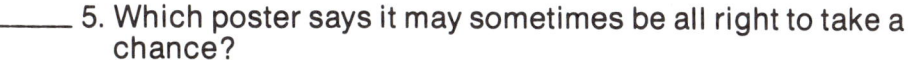

FINDING DETAILS IN A POSTER — 13

FIND THE FACTS

DIRECTIONS: Look for facts as you read this ad.

Would you like to be a detective? Buy the Super Detective Set! It comes complete with a real badge just like the one detectives carry. It has handcuffs and a whistle. It has ink for taking fingerprints. It has a magnifying glass that makes things look three times as big.

All of this can be yours for the low price of $2.95. If you don't love this set, just send it back within ten days. We'll send you back your money.

DIRECTIONS: You can find the facts in this ad. Fill in the blanks below to answer the questions.

1. What is this ad selling? _____

2. If you don't like the set, what can you do?
   _____
   _____

3. What four things besides the badge are in the set?
   a. _____ b. _____
   c. _____ d. _____

4. How much does the set cost?
   _____

5. How many times as big does the magnifying glass make things?
   _____

6. How many days does the ad give you to find out whether you like the set?
   _____

If you got at least three answers right, fill in the following award:

FINDING DETAILS IN AN ADVERTISEMENT — 15

THE GRAND CANYON

Each paragraph in the story below tells you some facts about the Grand Canyon.

> DIRECTIONS: Read the following paragraphs carefully. Below each paragraph are three facts. Some of the facts are found in the paragraph, and some of the facts are not. Put a check in front of sentences that tell facts that are in the paragraph. The first one is done for you.

1. A *canyon* is a narrow valley with high, steep sides. There is often a stream at the bottom of a canyon. The Grand Canyon is in the state of Arizona. It is one of the world's largest and most beautiful canyons.

    __✓__ a. This paragraph tells the meaning of the word *canyon*.

    _____ b. There is only one canyon in the world.

    __✓__ c. The Grand Canyon is in the state of Arizona.

2. The Grand Canyon was formed over millions of years. Water came down from the mountains and from rivers. It cut into the rock and dirt. This went on for years and years. As the water kept on running, it cut deeper into the rock. It cut through layers of rock. The layers are many colors. Some layers are red, purple, or black. Other layers are light brown.

    _____ a. The Grand Canyon was formed in only three years.

    _____ b. The Grand Canyon was made by running water.

    _____ c. The layers of rock in the Grand Canyon are many colors.

3. People who visit the Grand Canyon like to see its animals. Birds, beavers, sheep, lizards and mountain lions are some of the animals that live in the canyon. The Grand Canyon is the only place in the world that a special kind of squirrel called the *Kaibab squirrel* lives.

_____ a. Animals live in the Grand Canyon.

_____ b. Wolves live in the Grand Canyon.

_____ c. There is a zoo in the Grand Canyon.

4.   The United States has made the Grand Canyon a park. People from all over the world visit the park. There is a road that goes right into the canyon. This lets people see the canyon from a car or bus. Some people fly their own planes into and over the canyon. Still others like to camp in Grand Canyon National Park. Many people who visit the Grand Canyon say that it is one of the most beautiful spots in the world.

_____ a. You can visit the Grand Canyon by riding in a train.

_____ b. The Grand Canyon is a park in the United States.

_____ c. People are allowed to camp in the Grand Canyon.

FINDING FACTS IN A PARAGRAPH — 17

A BRIDGE OF FRIENDSHIP

> DIRECTIONS: Read each paragraph below. Then read the word groups after the paragraph. In the blank, write the word that makes each sentence true.

1. Almost a hundred years ago, a bridge was built across the St. Lawrence River. One side of the bridge was on land that belonged to the Mohawk Indians. The Mohawk Indians helped to build the bridge. They carried loads, dug ditches, and worked as helpers for other people.

    a. The Mohawk Indians helped to build a bridge across the _____ River.

    b. The Mohawk Indians worked as helpers for other people, carried loads, and dug _____.

2. The Mohawk Indians worked so hard that the bridge company wanted the Mohawks to work for them full-time. The company found that the Mohawk Indians were very brave. The bridge company trained twelve Indians to climb to high places. They learned to build high bridges and tall buildings. These Mohawks taught their families and friends what they had learned. Soon, there were seventy Mohawks able to work the high steel.

    a. The bridge company found that the Mohawks were very _____

    b. The Indians who had learned to work the high steel _____ their families and friends what they had learned.

18

3. The Mohawk Indians helped to build many bridges and big buildings. Young Mohawk boys began to climb the high steel when they were teenagers. The Mohawks built many bridges of steel all over the United States and Canada. But the most important bridge they built has no steel at all. It is the bridge of friendship that they have helped to build between Canada and the United States.

a. Mohawk boys learned about steelworking when they were _____.

b. _____ helped to build a bridge of friendship between the countries of Canada and the United States.

These pages have six answers for you to fill in. If you got at least four answers right, you have learned to find facts in paragraphs. You have earned the award below.

NAME _____

has proved he or she is an important expert at finding facts in a paragraph.

FINDING FACTS IN A PARAGRAPH — 19

GET THE PICTURE

Some details are more important to remember than others.

> DIRECTIONS: As you read this report, pretend that you just got a camera for your birthday. You want to know how to use it. Look for details that tell you how to use the camera.

Many people like to take photographs. Some people like pictures of friends, pets, or beautiful scenes. News photographers and advertisers take photos to help them in business. Many spacecraft have cameras. These cameras tell us more about our earth and outer space.

Maybe you would like to take pictures with a camera. The best camera to start out with is the *box camera*. Taking a picture with a box camera is easy. Stand at least two meters away from the person or thing that you are taking a photo of. Then look in the viewfinder. The viewfinder shows you exactly what will be in your snapshot. When you find the picture that you want in the viewfinder, press the shutter button gently. Now you've taken your first picture! Roll the film in the camera so that you are ready to take another picture. When you have taken a whole film roll of pictures, you can take the roll to a store to have it developed. When you get your pictures back, you can show your friends the pictures that you took all by yourself!

DIRECTIONS: You can find the important details from the report. Put a check beside each detail that you need to know to be able to take a picture.

____ 1. Some people take photos to help them in business.

____ 2. Many spacecraft have cameras.

____ 3. Stand at least two meters away from the subject of your photo.

____ 4. Find the picture you want in the viewfinder.

____ 5. Press the shutter button gently to take the picture.

____ 6. When you have taken a whole film roll of pictures, you can take the roll to a store to be developed.

____ 7. People enjoy seeing pictures of friends and pets.

A BRAVE PRINCESS

> DIRECTIONS: *Details* in a story often tell who, what, where, why, when, or how something happens. Look for details as you read this story.

Over three hundred years ago, when very few settlers lived in North America, there lived a young Indian princess by the name of Pocahontas. Pocahontas' father was named Powhatan. He was the chief of their Indian tribe.

One day Pocahontas saw Powhatan and some of his men bring a settler into camp. The settler's name was Captain John Smith. The Indians were very angry with this man. They were angry because they found Captain Smith on land that belonged to the Indians. The men pushed Captain Smith to the ground. They made him put his head on a rock. Pocahontas saw her father, Powhatan, raise a club into the air to hit the captain. Pocahontas knew that her father had lost his temper and could hurt Captain Smith. Quickly, Pocahontas put her own head between Captain Smith's head and the club. She begged her father not to hurt Captain Smith. Powhatan was so touched by his daughter's bravery that all of his anger was gone. He let Captain Smith go.

Pocahontas and Captain Smith became friends. She came to visit the town where the settlers lived. She became friends with many of the people in the town. One of the people that she met was John Rolfe.

Pocahontas and John fell in love. They got married. Later, they moved to England. People in England had heard about Pocahontas. They were excited to meet this brave Indian princess.

> DIRECTIONS: Write the missing fact in each sentence below. When you have finished, the sentences will be details from the story that tell *who*, *what*, *when*, *where*, *why*, and *how*.

1. This story took place _____ .
when?

2. The Indian princess' name is _____ .
who?

3. Powhatan was angry at Captain Smith because _____
why?
_____ .

4. Pocahontas saved Captain Smith's life by _____
how?
_____ .

5. Instead of hurting Captain Smith, Powhatan _____
what?
_____ .

6. After Pocahontas and John Rolfe were married, they traveled to _____ .
where?

FINDING FACTS IN A STORY

THE LONGEST DITCH IN THE WORLD

Have you ever dug a ditch to connect two puddles of water? If you have, you probably saw the water move easily from puddle to puddle. Ditches that connect water are called *canals*. The Suez Canal is the world's longest canal. It is in Egypt.

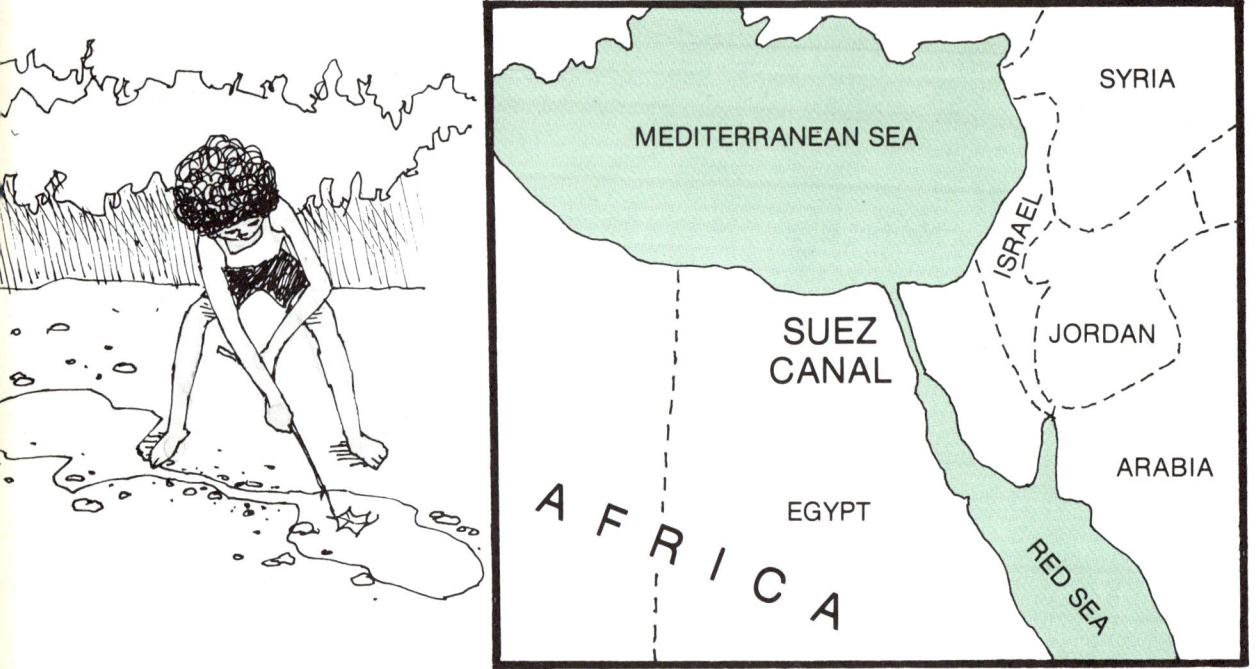

A Frenchman and his workers dug the canal about two hundred years ago. They dug the canal because they knew that a canal would save the sailors a lot of time. A ship could just go through the canal instead of sailing all the way around Africa.

Digging the canal was very hard. The Suez is a very hot place in which to work. There was no fresh water for the men to drink. A small canal had to be dug. The small canal brought drinking water to the workers. After the men got drinking water, they could dig the big canal.

Over the years, the Suez Canal has been dug deeper and wider. Today, the Suez Canal is very wide and deep. Even the largest supertankers can pass through it. Ships from countries all over the world use the canal every day.

DIRECTIONS: You can answer questions about the details in a story. Check the answer that best completes each sentence below.

1. The Suez Canal was dug

   ____ a. to bring fresh water to the desert.

   ____ b. so that people could sail between two ditches.

   ____ c. so ships wouldn't have to sail all the way around Africa.

2. Digging the canal was hard because

   ____ a. the people didn't want to work very hard.

   ____ b. the Suez is a hot, dry place.

   ____ c. the workers had to dig through rocks.

3. A smaller canal was dug before the big canal because

   ____ a. the smaller canal was needed to give workers water to drink.
   ____ b. the workers needed to practice digging a smaller canal before they dug the big one.
   ____ c. small boats could use the little canal while the workers were working on the big one.

4. By looking at the map, you can see that the Suez Canal goes between

   ____ a. the Mediterranean Sea and Egypt.

   ____ b. Africa and France.

   ____ c. the Mediterranean Sea and the Red Sea.

FINDING FACTS IN A STORY — 25

THE GREAT WALL OF CHINA

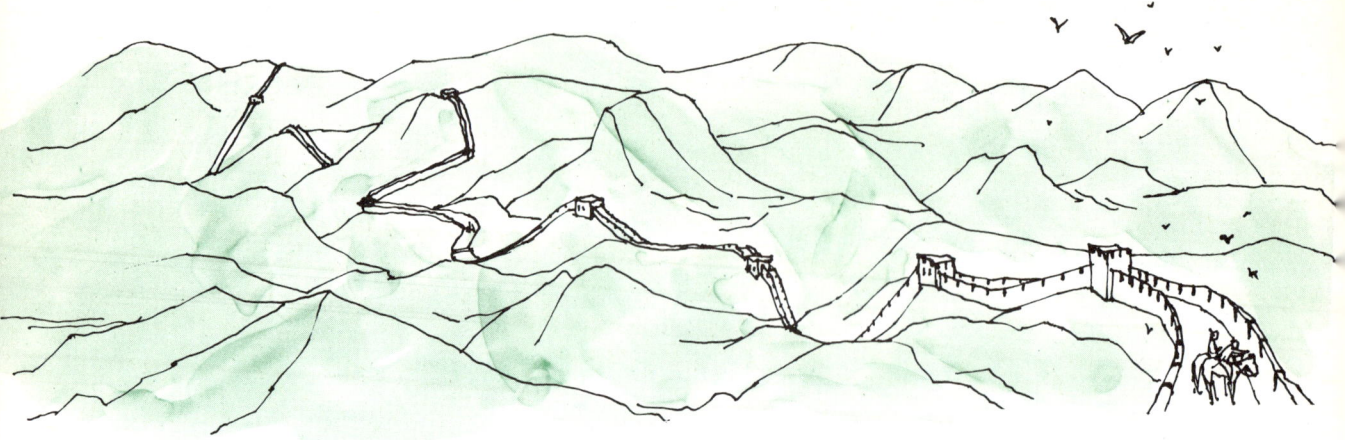

The first rockets that carried men into space flew very high. The men in the rockets looked back at the earth. They could see only one thing that had been built by people. It was the Great Wall of China.

The Great Wall of China is the longest building project ever made by man. The people of China built this long, strong wall to keep out the wild tribes who lived north of China.

The Great Wall was built about two thousand years ago. Back then, people had no machines to help them build. They had to build the wall by hand. It took them two hundred years to finish the wall. Many fathers, their sons, their grandsons, their great-grandsons, and their great-great-grandsons worked on this huge wall. The people of China built the wall well. It protected the Chinese for thousands of years.

A broad road runs along the top of the wall. Chinese soldiers on horses used to ride the road. All along the road were towers. Soldiers used to live in the towers. They could send messages to each other. They would send signals by smoke if it was daytime. The signals would be sent by fire if it was night.

Since airplanes and tanks have been invented, the Great Wall does not protect the people of China anymore. Soldiers no longer live in the towers. But people like to visit the Great Wall of China. They can look inside of the towers. They can walk on the road that runs along the top of the wall.

Now that you have read the story, you can find the details that are missing from the sentences below.

> DIRECTIONS: Complete each of the following sentences by writing the correct detail in the blank.

1. The Great Wall of China was built because the Chinese wanted to keep out _____ .

2. The Great Wall is about _____ years old.

3. The wall took about _____ years to build.

4. A broad _____ runs along the top of the wall.

5. _____ used the road.

6. The soldiers would send signals by _____ if it was daytime.

7. Today, people like to _____ the Great Wall of China.

FINDING FACTS IN A STORY — 27

BUILDING A TREE HOUSE

Jean decided to build a tree house. Her dad said that he would help her.

"Go into the house. Collect all the things that we will need to build the tree house," said Dad.

Jean went into the house. She thought about the things that she and her father would need to build the tree house.

> DIRECTIONS: You can help Jean decide what tools and building materials will be needed to build Jean's tree house. Put a check in front of each item that Jean and her dad will need.

_____ 1. nails

_____ 2. scissors

_____ 3. clock

_____ 4. saw

_____ 5. spoon

_____ 6. boards

_____ 7. paper clips

_____ 8. hammer

_____ 9. bedspread

_____ 10. water colors

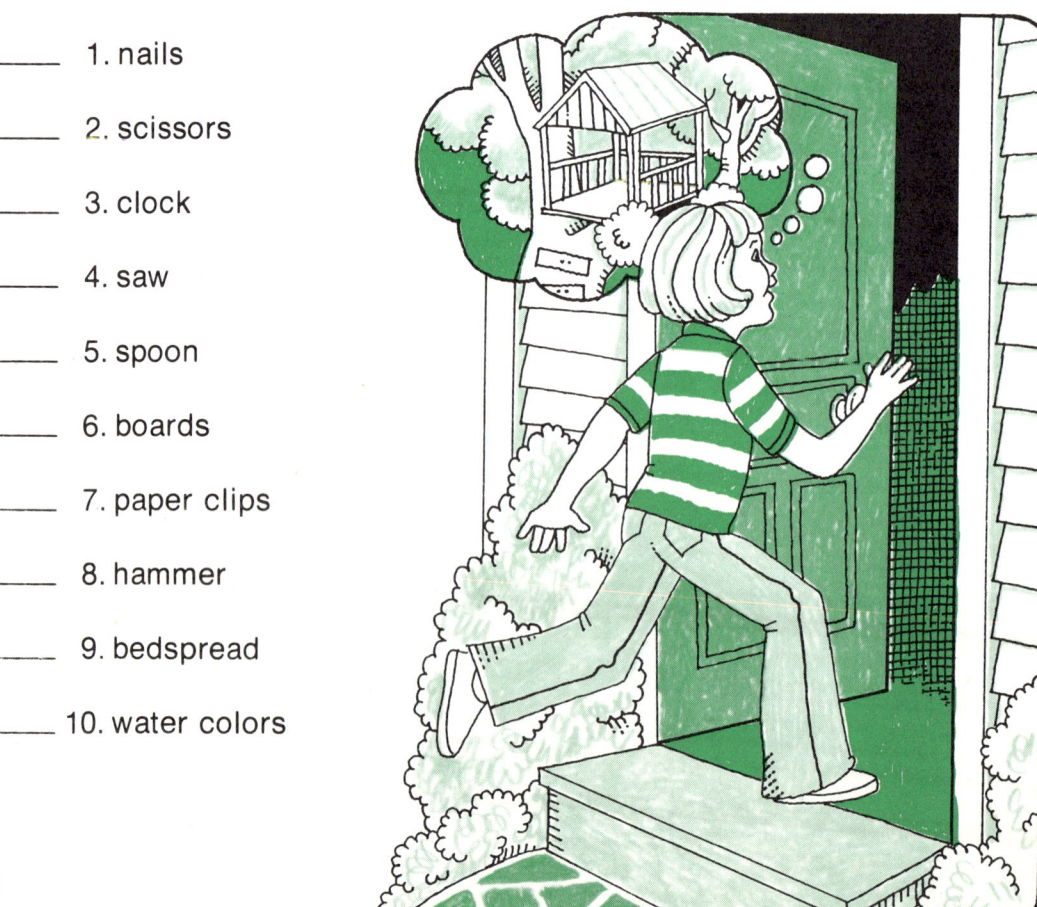

ASKING IMPORTANT QUESTIONS

Have you ever bought something in a store? If you have, you know how important it is to get the facts before you buy.

Let's say that you are in a store to buy a record player. You have found one that you can afford. But before you buy the record player, you want to ask the clerk some questions.

DIRECTIONS: Put a check before the questions that are important to ask before you buy the record player.

_____ 1. Was the record player shipped to the store in a red truck?

_____ 2. Can I get my money back if I don't like the record player?

_____ 3. If the record player breaks, are parts easy to get?

_____ 4. Did the record player arrive at the store on Tuesday?

_____ 5. Can the record player play both big records and small records?

_____ 6. How old is the clerk?

_____ 7. How big was the truck in which the record player was shipped?

_____ 8. Does the record player have a good needle?

RECOGNIZING SIGNIFICANT DETAILS — 29

BIRD MAN

John Audubon was born about two hundred years ago. The house that he lived in was in the country. His next-door neighbor was a scientist who studied nature. John and his neighbor often hiked through woods and fields. They watched the wild animals. They found out what food the animals ate, and saw where each animal lived and how it acted.

Of all the animals, John loved to watch the birds the most. He watched the birds as they soared through the air. He drew pictures of many kinds of birds. He noticed the kind of nest that each bird lived in. He watched the birds take care of their young and find food.

When John Audubon was twenty-three, he got married. He opened a store. Even though he was in business, John still spent most of his time drawing birds.

Soon he had lost so much money that he had to give up his business. He was sent to jail because he couldn't pay his bills. The sheriff took everything away from John Audubon but his bird drawings. No one thought that his drawings were worth anything.

When he got out of jail, John Audubon was very poor. But John's wife, Lucy, believed that he was a great artist. She helped John by working as a schoolteacher for some rich children. In this way, the family would have some money, and John could still paint.

Now John Audubon worked very hard. He finished hundreds of bird paintings. The paintings were in full color. The birds were painted the size that they are in real life. He drew true-to-life pictures of birds flying through the air, nesting, or feeding their young. He kept studying and painting birds until he had painted beautiful pictures of all of the birds that live in North America.

John Audubon had his paintings printed in a book. Scientists and writers were amazed when they saw the book. It was beautiful. All of the birds were shown in settings as they would be found in nature. John Audubon became famous. Even today, his books are used by people who study birds.

> DIRECTIONS: Write an *A* before each fact that agrees with what the story says. Write an *N* before each fact that does not agree with what the story says. The first one is done for you.

a 1. John Audubon was an artist.

____ 2. John Audubon is best known for his dog pictures.

____ 3. Audubon was interested in watching the habits of birds.

____ 4. Audubon and his store did well in business.

____ 5. Audubon was sent to jail for stealing.

____ 6. Lucy, John's wife, worked as a schoolteacher.

____ 7. Audubon painted beautiful pictures of all of the birds that live in Australia.

____ 8. John Audubon had his paintings printed in a book.

FINDING FACTS IN A STORY — 31

HARRIET TUBMAN

Harriet Tubman was born a slave. She didn't get a chance to go to school. As a child, Harriet had to work very hard in the fields all day. That way, her owner could make a lot of money when he sold his crops. Harriet didn't think that she was being treated fairly.

When Harriet grew up, she escaped from the plantation. She ran away to the northern United States. There, and in Canada, black people could be free.

Harriet liked to be free. She felt sorry for all of the black people who were still slaves.

Harriet returned to the South to rescue other slaves. She helped them to escape. She made sure that they made it north, to freedom.

Harriet was in great danger because of a law that had just been passed. The law said it was a crime to help runaway slaves. She also found out that the slave-catchers said that they would pay $40,000 to anyone who could catch Harriet Tubman.

Harriet was clever. She outsmarted the slave-catchers. She found out about a group that would help her rescue slaves in secret. The group was called the *Underground Railroad*. People who belonged to the Underground Railroad hid Harriet and the other runaway slaves in their houses. That made it harder for slave-catchers to find the escaped slaves.

Harriet had many exciting adventures while helping slaves escape. In all, she made nineteen trips back to the South. She guided about three hundred slaves to freedom.

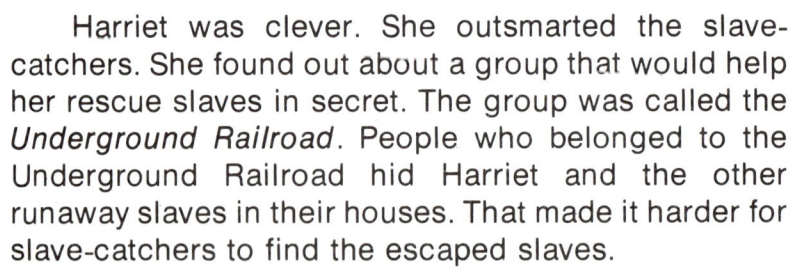

Then, war broke out in the United States. It was called the Civil War. The northern states fought with the southern states. Harriet was on the side of the northern states because they believed that slaves should be free. Harriet worked hard for the northern army. She worked as a nurse and as a scout for raiding parties. She also spied behind enemy lines. After four years, the Civil War was over. The northern states won. All the slaves were freed.

Harriet Tubman went to her home in Auburn, New York. She helped raise money so that black children could go to school. She also helped start a special home that took good care of older black people.

After Harriet Tubman died, a monument was built in honor of this bold, fearless woman who helped so many people win their freedom.

> DIRECTIONS: Write an *A* before the facts that *agree* with the story. Write an *N* before the facts that do *not* agree with the story. Write an *M* before the facts that *might* be true, but are not part of the story. The first one is done for you.

a 1. Harriet Tubman was born a slave.

_____ 2. Harriet thought that slavery was fair.

_____ 3. In 1857, Harriet led her parents to freedom.

_____ 4. The Underground Railroad helped Harriet lead slaves to freedom.

_____ 5. The book *Freedom Train: The Story of Harriet Tubman*, by Dorothy Sterling, tells more about Harriet Tubman.

_____ 6. Harriet was a spy during the Civil War.

FINDING FACTS IN A STORY — 33

THE GREAT PYRAMID

1. Picture in your mind a building big enough to cover eight football fields. Can you picture this building forty stories high? A building like this was built before machines were invented. The building was built over 4,500 years ago. It is called the *Great Pyramid*.

2. We do not know just how the Egyptians built pyramids. But very old drawings show one idea of how the Great Pyramid may have been built. First, the Egyptians built roads to the spot where they would build a pyramid. Then they cut the stones for the pyramid. The stones were moved along the road on wooden rollers. When the stones got to the building site, they were stacked on top of each other. The last step was to put a pointed stone at the very top of the pyramid.

3. The Great Pyramid took over two million blocks of stone to build. Some people think that 400,000 men worked for twenty years to finish the Great Pyramid.

4. You may wonder what this huge building was used for. Strange as it may seem, the Great Pyramid was built as a place to bury an Egyptian king when he died. The people that lived in Egypt long ago believed that when a person died, it was important to protect the person's body. They thought that this would make the person's spirit live on. When the king died, the people buried him in the Great Pyramid to protect his body. The body was buried in a secret room inside the pyramid. Gold, jewels, statues, and gifts were buried with the body.

The story you just read has four paragraphs. Each one tells many facts about the Great Pyramid. You can tell which facts come from which paragraph.

> DIRECTIONS: Read each question below. In the blank, write the number of the paragraph that answers the question.

_____ 1. Which paragraph tells how many stones were needed to build the pyramid?

_____ 2. Which paragraph tells how wide and tall the Great Pyramid is?

_____ 3. Which paragraph tells how the Great Pyramid may have been built?

_____ 4. Which paragraph tells why the Great Pyramid was built?

_____ 5. Which paragraph tells when the Great Pyramid was built?

_____ 6. Which paragraph tells about the secret room inside the pyramid?

Check your answers. Did you get at least four answers right? _____ If your answer is yes, fill out your award below.

FINDING FACTS IN A STORY — 35

THE LEANING TOWER OF PISA

There is a surprising old bell tower in Pisa, Italy. It is different from any tower in the world. This tower leans so far over that it looks like it will fall down. But the tower was built about seven hundred years ago. It hasn't fallen yet.

Before the tower was built, the townspeople saved their money for many years. Finally, the building was started. The tower was built of beautiful, white marble. It took almost two hundred years to build the tower.

But there was something about the ground under the tower that the builders didn't know. Part of the ground that the tower was built over was soft. The part of the tower under the soft ground began to sink. The tower leaned to one side instead of standing straight up and down as other buildings do.

The people in the town of Pisa tried to fix their beautiful tower. They found out that the ground was soft because there was water in the soil. The people tried to pump the water out of the ground. The pumping didn't work. The tower kept leaning over more and more.

Builders now say that the tower can never be fixed. They can't make it straight up and down.

Today, the leaning tower of Pisa is famous. People from all over the world come to see this beautiful, slanting bell tower.

Sometimes the order in which things happen is important. Now that you have read about the leaning tower of Pisa, you can put the events from the story in the right order.

> DIRECTIONS: Each exercise below has two sentences. For each exercise, draw a circle around the sentence that tells what happened first. The first one is done for you.

1. a. The town got the money to build the tower. *(circled)*

   b. The tower was carefully built of beautiful, white marble.

2. a. The ground under the tower was soft.

   b. The tower began to lean over.

3. a. The people tried to pump the water out of the ground.

   b. The people of Pisa found out that the ground was soft because there was water in the soil.

4. a. The tower was built about seven hundred years ago.

   b. Today, builders say that the tower can never be fixed.

DETERMINING THE SEQUENCE OF FACTS — 37

INVISIBLE WRITING

Now you see it — now you don't. One minute, you're holding a blank piece of paper. All at once, there's a message on it! Magic? No, it's invisible ink.

Invisible ink has been used for many years for secret writing. Spies use it to send secret letters. The people the spies are trying to fool see only blank paper. The friends of the spies know how to bring out the writing.

Here is how to write with invisible ink. First, get together everything that you will need. Get some milk or lemon juice, a small stick, a blank piece of paper, and a lamp.

Now wet the stick with the milk or lemon juice. Write your message on the paper with the wet stick. Let the paper dry.

Now give the "blank" piece of paper to your friend. Let your friend bring out the writing. The friend can do this by holding the piece of paper over the turned-on light bulb of the lamp. Have your friend hold the paper so that the side that is written on is nearest the heat. After a few minutes, your friend can turn the paper over. As if by magic, your secret message will appear!

DIRECTIONS: You can put the steps below in the order that you should follow to send a message in invisible ink. Write a 1 beside the step you should do first. Write a 2 beside the step that you should do second, and so on. The first one is done for you.

a. _____ Let the paper dry.

b. _____ Wet the stick with the milk or lemon juice.

c. _____ Give the paper that has the invisible writing on it to your friend.

d. __1__ Get all the supplies together that you will need to send your message.

e. _____ Write your message.

f. _____ Have the friend hold the piece of paper over a turned-on light bulb.

g. _____ Now your friend can read your message.

DETERMINING THE SEQUENCE OF FACTS — 39

FIND THE DIFFERENCE

These two pictures show a girl dressed in different holiday costumes. You can tell how the two pictures are different.

DIRECTIONS: Write an *H* in front of each word group that tells about the Halloween picture. Write a *T* in front of each word group that tells about the Thanksgiving picture. The first one is done for you.

__H__ 1. has a pointed hat

_____ 2. wearing an apron

_____ 3. carrying a jack-o-lantern

_____ 4. carrying a broom

_____ 5. has a turkey

_____ 6. carrying corn

_____ 7. has long hair

Picture A

Picture B

> DIRECTIONS: Look at picture A and picture B. Think about how the pictures are alike and how they are different. Then read the story about the two pictures. As you read, fill in each blank by writing *A* or *B*.

The pictures above are alike in some ways. The pictures are alike because they are both drawings of aircraft. Both pictures have people in them.

The pictures are also different in some ways. The aircraft in picture ____ is in the air, but the aircraft in picture ____ is on the ground. In
   1   2
picture ____, some people are getting on the aircraft, but in picture
        3
____, people are just watching the aircraft. The aircraft in picture ____
4   5
is at an airport. The aircraft in picture ____ is not. People will be riding in
                                                      6
the aircraft in picture ____. We don't know who is riding on the aircraft
                                7
in picture ____.
            8

COMPARING FACTS IN A PICTURE — 41

TWO QUEENS

There have been many queens in history. Two of the most famous queens were Cleopatra and Victoria. Each of these women led her nation for many years. Each woman was only eighteen when she became queen.

During Cleopatra's twenty-one years as queen of Egypt, her army lost a battle to the Romans. But Cleopatra was clever. Even though the Romans defeated her army, she still ran her country. Stories, poems, and plays have been written about this great woman.

Queen Victoria ruled England for sixty-three years. She was one of the greatest rulers that England ever had. Victoria set a good example for her people. She was modest, smart, and a hard worker. When Victoria was queen, England fought and won many wars. A law was passed that made conditions better for people who worked. Another law gave every child the right to go to school. Victoria also made sure that England sold and bought many products from other countries.

DIRECTIONS: You can tell how the two queens are alike, and how they are different. Below are some facts from the story. Write a *C* in front of each sentence that tells about Queen Cleopatra. Write a *V* in front of each sentence that tells about Queen Victoria. Write both *C* and *V* in front of each sentence that tells about both queens. The first one is done for you.

C 1. She was queen of Egypt.

____ 2. She ruled for sixty-three years.

____ 3. She was eighteen when she became queen.

____ 4. Her army lost a battle to the Romans.

____ 5. She ruled for twenty-one years.

____ 6. She led her nation.

____ 7. She set a good example for her people.

____ 8. Her country passed many good laws while she was queen.

Did you get at least six answers right? ____
If your answer is yes, fill out your award below.

NAME _____ has shown that he or she knows how things are alike and how they are different.

COMPARING FACTS IN AN ARTICLE — 43

UNCOVERING HIDDEN FACTS

Did you know that some facts are hidden in stories? You can only uncover these facts if you think carefully about what you've read. See if you can guess the hidden facts in the following stories.

> DIRECTIONS: Read each story. Use the facts in the story to find the correct ending to each sentence below. Put a check in front of the correct ending. The first one is done for you.

1. Jeff and Don were at the swimming pool. They practiced diving into the pool.

    Jeff and Don were wearing

    ____ a. a halloween costume

    ✓ b. swimming trunks

    ____ c. pajamas

2. Laurel looked out of the window. She saw big clouds of smoke darken the sky. She saw a red truck race down the street. Its siren was wailing.

    The red truck was

    ____ a. a pickup truck

    ____ b. a moving van

    ____ c. a fire engine

3. Mr. Day's class went on a field trip. Don and Ben watched an elephant eat some peanuts. Steve saw a huge black snake. Cathy got to feed the llama.

Mr. Day's class went to

_____ a. a farm

_____ b. the zoo

_____ c. the pet store

4. Anna was on her way to school. She was wearing boots and a raincoat. She was also carrying an umbrella. As she walked along, she heard a distant rumble in the sky. She saw some lightning.

The weather that day was

_____ a. rainy

_____ b. icy

_____ c. hot

5. Bob and some friends met at the park. Tom brought his ball. The boys divided themselves into two teams. They started playing. Bob played very well. He made three baskets in a row.

The boys were playing

_____ a. dodge ball

_____ b. basketball

_____ c. handball

INFERRING FACTS — 45

PUZZLING QUESTIONS

When you solve riddles, you are uncovering hidden facts.

> **DIRECTIONS:** Read each riddle. The answers are listed below. When you find the answer to a riddle, write it on the line.

the leaves of a book   this book, of course
Harriet   a tower of Pisa
a detail   Suez

1. What kind of tail tells facts about a story?
   _____

2. What kind of leaves don't come off the trees in the fall?
   _____

   _____

3. Mike called the restaurant and ordered twenty-three pizzas to take home. When Mike got to the restaurant, what did he find?
   _____

   _____

4. Did Mike, Harry, or Sue eat the most pizza?
   _____

5. Is Mike, Harry, or Sue the best singer?
   _____

6. What has forty-eight pages and tells how to work with facts and details?
   _____

Some of these riddles are hard. If you got one right, fill in the award below.

46 — INFERRING FACTS